M000214588

THE TOMATO KETCHUP BOOK

THE
TOMATO
KETCHUP
BOOK

INTRODUCTION

Whether you dip, spread, splodge or stir, there's no denying that Heinz Tomato Ketchup occupies a special place in all our hearts. So in this book, we've decided to celebrate this beloved condiment in all its tomatoey glory, with a collection of delicious recipes, along with heaps of fun facts and stunning stats that reveal the history of everyone's favourite sauce.

Whether you want to jazz up a cheese toastie or add a special touch to a delicious risotto, the meal ideas will keep your whole family happy, while the insider knowledge and fascinating facts are sure to impress at your next pub quiz. So if you've ever wondered where the name 'ketchup' comes from, or wanted to know which sauce is favoured by NASA's top astronauts, read on.

A BRIEF HISTORY OF HEINZ TOMATO KETCHUP

In 1869, Henry John Heinz founded a company selling bottles of horseradish sauce based on his mother's recipe. He was only 25, but even this wasn't his first foray into business. He'd started selling produce from the family garden at the age of eight.

When his horseradish business folded, Henry J. Heinz enlisted the help of his brother John and cousin Frederick, and started selling ketchup in 1876. At first it was called 'catsup', but he switched to the spelling 'ketchup' in the 1880s.

In 1886, Henry started selling his products in the UK, too, and by 1907 Heinz products were being sold all over the world. The Heinz repertoire quickly expanded to include a huge range of delicious foods, including pickles, baked beans, mustards and preserves.

In the 1920s, Heinz expanded its production to the UK, and later became an important food supplier during the Second World War (although Heinz Tomato Ketchup briefly disappeared from shelves at this time due to wartime supply issues).

In 1951, Heinz was granted the Royal Warrant, a prestigious honour that the company still holds today.

It's now been over 150 years since Henry J. Heinz made his first forays into the world of sauces and preserves, and his iconic ketchup bottles remain a key item in kitchen cupboards all over the world.

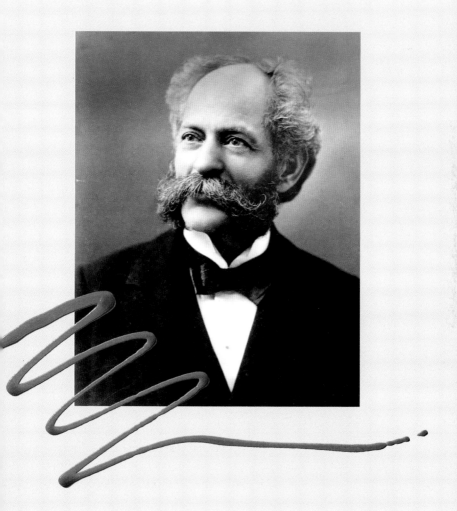

HEINZ TOMATO KETCHUP TIMELINE

Henry J. Heinz starts selling bottles of horseradish sauce.

Heinz Tomato Ketchup is brought to the UK and sold by Fortnum & Mason.

The London branch of H.J. Heinz moved to premises in Farringdon Road.

13 million bottles of Heinz Tomato Ketchup are now being sold worldwide, exported to India, Australia, South America, Japan, Indonesia, New Zealand, South Africa and the UK.

| 1869 | 1876 | 1886 | 1890 | 1898 | 1904 | 1907 |

Heinz Tomato Ketchup launches in the US.

Heinz patents the iconic octagonal glass bottle.

After years of research, Heinz develops a recipe for a preservative-free tomato ketchup.

The visionary Henry J. Heinz dies and his son Howard takes over the company.

Heinz Tomato Ketchup briefly disappears from British shelves due to shortages in the Second World War.

The 'Top Down' bottle is launched.

After 150 years of deliciousness, Heinz Tomato Ketchup remains a firm favourite, with 650 million bottles sold every year.

1919 **1920** **1939** **1951** **2003** **2018** TODAY

Heinz production expands to the UK.

Heinz receives the Royal Warrant, becoming official purveyors of goods to her majesty Queen Elizabeth II.

Heinz launches its No Added Salt & Sugar Tomato Ketchup.

11

EGGY BREAD

VEGETARIAN OPTION
PREP 5 MINUTES
COOK 10 MINUTES

6 large free-range eggs
2 tbsp Heinz Tomato Ketchup, plus extra to serve
50ml whole milk
2 tsp dried oregano
50g Parmesan or vegetarian hard cheese, finely grated
salt and pepper
50g butter
8 slices of white or brown bread
crispy bacon and/or pan-fried mushrooms, to serve

Crack the eggs into a wide, shallow bowl. Whisk well with a fork until the whites and the yolks are fully combined. Add the ketchup, milk, dried oregano, grated cheese and plenty of seasoning. Whisk again until well combined.

Preheat the oven to 120°C/100°C fan/gas mark ½.

Melt half the butter in a large, non-stick frying pan over a medium heat. One at a time, dip four slices of bread into the egg mixture, so that they get completely coated, then lay into the pan. Cook for 1–2 minutes on each side until crisp and golden brown. Transfer to a roasting tray and put in the oven to keep warm. Repeat with the remaining bread slices.

Serve the eggy bread with more ketchup, crispy bacon and/or pan-fried mushrooms.

PRAWN COCKTAIL SALAD

PREP 20 MINUTES

4 tbsp Heinz [Seriously Good] Mayonnaise

2 tbsp Heinz Tomato Ketchup

1–2 tbsp hot sauce (we like sriracha)

zest and juice of 1 lemon

salt and pepper

300g sustainably sourced cooked and peeled king prawns

2 baby gem lettuces, leaves separated and core sliced

1 cucumber, peeled into long ribbons, core chopped

2 ripe avocados, sliced

small handful of chives, snipped

In a large bowl, mix together the mayonnaise, ketchup, 1 tablespoon of the hot sauce, all the lemon zest and half the lemon juice. Season to taste, adding more hot sauce if you like it spicy.

Add the prawns, sliced lettuce core and chopped cucumber core to the dressing. Toss together so that the prawns become completely coated in the cocktail sauce.

Lay the lettuce leaves, the avocado slices and the cucumber ribbons onto a large platter or four plates. Squeeze over the remaining lemon juice and season with salt and pepper. Pile the prawn cocktail into the middle of the salad, then scatter over the chives to serve.

THE HEINZ TOMATO KETCHUP BOTTLE

At the time Heinz first started selling sauces, brown bottles were far more common, and were often used to cover up the contents and hide any potential impurities. Henry wanted to showcase the high quality of his ingredients, so he opted for a transparent glass bottle so that the contents were clearly visible.

The Heinz Tomato Ketchup bottle went through a few changes in the early years, but the iconic octagonal Heinz bottle we know and love today was patented in 1890, while the familiar keystone design first appeared on labels between 1887 and 1895.

The Heinz Tomato Ketchup bottle was designed with a narrower neck than other bottles to prevent too much air getting into the bottle and browning the ketchup.

The classic glass bottle remains popular today, but in 2003 Heinz also launched the 'upside down' squeezy bottle – the Top Down Bottle – for those who just can't wait a second to get their hit of ketchupy goodness.

In 2009, the Heinz Tomato Ketchup label was redesigned, with the original pickle being swapped for an illustration of a vine-ripened tomato.

1880–1905 1889–1894 1887–1895 1889–1910 1906–1910

CHEAT'S CURRYWURST HOT DOGS

PREP 5 MINUTES
COOK 30 MINUTES

4 jumbo hot dogs
4 large hot dog rolls, split
   down the middle

For the caramelised onions
2 large onions, finely sliced
250ml water
2 tbsp olive oil
salt
1 tbsp Heinz Tomato Ketchup

For the cheat's currywurst
*   sauce*
5 tbsp Heinz Tomato Ketchup
2 tsp medium curry powder
1 tsp smoked paprika
½ tsp garlic granules
2–3 tbsp water
salt and pepper

Put the onions into a medium saucepan over a medium heat. Pour in the 250ml water. Cook for 20 minutes or so until all the water has evaporated and the onions have collapsed.

Increase the heat to medium–high, then add the olive oil and a good pinch of salt. Fry, stirring regularly, for 10 minutes, until the onions are beginning to caramelise. Stir through 1 tablespoon of the ketchup, then cook for a further 5 minutes until sticky and golden.

For the cheat's currywurst sauce, mix together the ketchup, curry powder, smoked paprika and garlic granules in a small bowl. Add the water until the sauce is a drizzling consistency. Season to taste.

Cook the hot dogs according to the packet instructions. Reheat the onions.

Divide the onions between the four rolls, top with the cooked hot dogs, then spoon over the cheat's currywurst sauce and serve.

The caramelised onions can be made the day before and kept in the fridge.

VEGGIE COTTAGE PIE

SERVES 4–6

VEGETARIAN
PREP 10 MINUTES
COOK 1 HOUR

20g dried porcini mushrooms
250ml boiling water
2 tbsp olive oil
1 large red onion, finely
    chopped
2 carrots, peeled and finely
    chopped
2 celery stalks, finely chopped
salt and pepper
3 garlic cloves, finely chopped
2 x 400g tins plum tomatoes
2 x 400g tins green lentils,
    drained
a few thyme sprigs, leaves
    stripped
2 tbsp Heinz Tomato Ketchup
1 tsp yeast extract
750g floury potatoes (we
    like Maris Piper or King
    Edwards), peeled and cut
    in half
75g butter
50g extra-mature Cheddar,
    grated
buttered peas, to serve

Preheat the oven to 200°C/180°C fan/gas mark 6.

Put the dried porcini mushrooms into a bowl, pour over the boiling water and leave to soak.

Meanwhile, heat the oil in a large saucepan over a medium heat. Add the onion, carrots and celery, along with a pinch of salt. Cook, stirring occasionally, for 8-10 minutes until softened but not coloured. Add the garlic and cook for a further 30 seconds, then tip in the tomatoes and lentils. Add most of the thyme, along with all the ketchup and yeast extract. Add the porcini mushrooms, along with their soaking liquid. Give everything a good mix, then bring to a simmer and leave to bubble away while you make the mash.

Put the potatoes into a large saucepan of cold salted water. Bring to the boil, then cook for 20 minutes until tender. Drain, then leave to steam dry for a few minutes. Tip the cooked potatoes back into the pan. Add the butter and remaining thyme, along with plenty of salt and pepper, then mash using a potato masher.

Season the lentil filling to taste, then spoon into a medium baking dish. Spread the mash on top, then scatter over the grated cheese. Bake for 20 minutes until the pie is bubbling and the top is golden. Leave to cool for 5 minutes before serving. We like to eat this with some buttered peas.

CHILLI CHEESE TOASTIE

VEGETARIAN
PREP 5 MINUTES
COOK 6 MINUTES

small piece of fresh ginger,
  peeled
1 green chilli, finely chopped
1 tbsp Heinz Tomato Ketchup,
  plus extra to serve
2 tsp curry powder
1 tsp cumin seeds
1 spring onion, finely sliced
  (both green and white
  parts)
100g extra-mature Cheddar,
  grated
25g softened butter
4 thick slices of white bread

Finely grate the ginger into a bowl, then add the chilli, ketchup, curry powder, cumin seeds, spring onion and grated Cheddar. Mix well so that the cheese gets coated in all the spices.

Spread a little of the butter across one side of each bread slice. Melt the remaining butter in a non-stick frying pan over a medium–high heat.

Lay two slices of bread, butter-side down, into the pan. Divide the cheese filling between both, then sandwich together with the remaining bread slices, butter-side up.

Fry the chilli cheese toasties for 2–3 minutes on each side, using a fish slice to squash the sandwiches together while they cook.

Cut each toastie in half, then serve with more ketchup for dipping.

KETCHUP FACTS

In 1893, H.J. Heinz was behind one of the biggest ever promotional give-aways at the Chicago World Fair. Upon discovering that the Heinz exhibition space was to be on the second floor, away from the main attractions, Heinz announced they would be giving away limited-edition pickle charms (based on the famous Heinz pickle, which featured on many product labels, including the Heinz Tomato Ketchup bottle). His plan paid off – swarms of customers climbed the stairs to view the Heinz exhibition, and almost **1 million pickle charms** were given away.

Heinz Tomato Ketchup was first sold in the UK in 1886 at London's prestigious department store Fortnum & Mason. H. J. Heinz visited the store in person to present his products: after tasting what he had to offer, Fortnum's head of Grocery and Purchasing famously shook his hand and said:

'I think, Mr Heinz, we'll take the lot.'

In 1900, Heinz was the first company to install an electric sign in New York City. Featuring an enormous Heinz pickle, the sign was **13 metres high.**

CHEESEBURGER FRIES

PREP 5 MINUTES
COOK 35 MINUTES

1kg frozen French fries
1 tbsp olive oil
500g good-quality beef mince
1 onion, finely chopped
salt and pepper
2 tsp garlic granules
2 tsp celery salt
6 cheese slices
3 tbsp Heinz Tomato Ketchup
3 tbsp Heinz [Seriously Good]
   Mayonnaise
¼ iceberg lettuce, shredded
4 gherkins, roughly chopped
   or 8 slices pickled jalapeños

Preheat the oven to 200°C/180°C fan/gas mark 6.

Tip out the fries on to a large roasting tray. Spread in a single layer so that they evenly crisp. Roast in the oven for 25–30 minutes, flipping halfway, until crisp and golden.

Meanwhile, heat the olive oil in a frying pan over a medium–high heat. Add the beef mince and onion, along with a good pinch of salt. Fry for 15–18 minutes, breaking down the mince with the back of your spoon and then stirring regularly, until the mince is cooked through and browned. If the meat sticks to the pan, you can add a splash of water to loosen it.

Stir in the garlic granules and celery salt. Season the mince with black pepper to taste. Cook for 1 minute, then remove the pan from the heat.

Once the fries are cooked and out of the oven, turn the grill to high.

Pile the beef mince on top of the fries, then top with the cheese slices. Slide back under the grill for 2–3 minutes until the cheese is melted.

Squirt over the ketchup and mayonnaise, then scatter the lettuce and gherkins or jalapeños over the top of the cheeseburger fries. Bring to the table for everyone to help themselves.

THE NUMBER
57

Mr. Heinz thought of a number!

If you're looking for a cheeky way to speed up your ketchup, try tapping on the '57' on your Heinz Tomato Ketchup label. This 'sweet spot' helps release the ketchup from the bottle.

The famous number 57 that appears on every Heinz Tomato Ketchup bottle has a slightly unusual history. Henry J. Heinz was impressed by an advert he saw for a shoe company that talked about having more than 21 types of shoe. He decided to do something similar, but hit on the number 57 – some people say it's because his wife's favourite number was five, and his was seven – even though there were more than 60 Heinz products by 1896, when the '57 varieties' concept was created.

WARTIME SHORTAGES

During the Second World War, tomato supplies to the UK were cut off, meaning Heinz Tomato Ketchup was temporarily off the menu. Brits had to rely on salad cream (luckily, Heinz had that covered too). It took until 1948 for Heinz Tomato Ketchup to reappear on British shelves: a nine-year ketchup drought. It's easy to imagine how excited ketchup-lovers were when their favourite sauce returned!

PIZZA PINWHEELS

MAKES
8

PREP 5 MINUTES
COOK 15 MINUTES

320g ready-rolled puff pastry
**4 tbsp Heinz Tomato
  Ketchup, plus extra to
  serve**
8 slices salami
2 tsp dried oregano
100g grated mozzarella
1 medium free-range egg

You will need a pastry brush.

Unravel the sheet of puff pastry. Leaving a 1cm border around the edges, spread with the ketchup, then lay over the salami slices and sprinkle 1 teaspoon of the dried oregano and the grated mozzarella on top.

Starting with one of the shorter ends, roll the pastry up as tight as possible into a log – you can use the paper to help you. Put in the fridge to chill for 20 minutes.

Preheat the oven to 200°C/180°C fan/gas mark 6. Line a large baking tray with baking paper.

Using a sharp serrated knife, cut the roll into eight equal slices. Place, swirl facing up, on to the lined baking tray.

Crack the egg into a small bowl, then whisk well with a fork until the white and yolk are fully combined.

Brush the pizza pinwheels with the beaten egg, then sprinkle over the remaining 1 teaspoon of oregano. Bake in the oven for 15 minutes until puffed up and golden. Leave to cool for 5 minutes before tucking in. Serve with extra ketchup, for dipping, if you like.

KETCHUP CHICKEN

PREP 10 MINUTES
COOK 45 MINUTES

1kg free-range skin-on, bone-in chicken thighs and drumsticks

2 tbsp rapeseed or vegetable oil

salt and pepper

2 fat garlic cloves

thumb-sized piece of fresh ginger, peeled

2–3 tsp dried chilli flakes (depending on how spicy you like it)

4 tbsp Heinz Tomato Ketchup

1 tbsp soy sauce

1 tbsp soft light brown sugar

3 tbsp warm water

Preheat the oven to 200°C/180°C fan/gas mark 6. Line your largest roasting tin with kitchen foil.

In the tin, toss the chicken pieces in the oil and plenty of seasoning, then spread out in an even layer so that each piece cooks evenly. Roast for 25 minutes.

Meanwhile, finely grate the garlic and ginger into a bowl. Add the chilli flakes, ketchup, soy sauce, brown sugar and water. Stir until the sugar has dissolved.

After the chicken has cooked for 25 minutes, remove from the oven and pour the sauce over the top, then toss to coat. Return to the oven for a further 15–20 minutes, basting halfway, until the chicken is cooked through, sticky and caramelised. Serve and enjoy.

CHICKEN BURGER

PREP 10 MINUTES
COOK 10 MINUTES

2 free-range skinless,
    boneless chicken breasts
salt and pepper
2 brioche or seeded burger
    buns, halved
2 tbsp Heinz Tomato Ketchup
1 roasted pepper from a jar,
    drained and finely sliced
½ baby gem lettuce, shredded
50g feta, crumbled
4 slices pickled jalapeños

For the sauce
1 garlic clove, crushed
2 tbsp Heinz Tomato Ketchup
2 tsp Cajun seasoning
1 tbsp olive oil

*You will need a rolling pin and
    a pastry brush.*

In a small bowl, mix together the sauce ingredients, then set aside.

Take out two large pieces of baking paper. Place a piece of baking paper on to your work surface. Season the chicken breasts on both sides with salt and pepper, then lay on top of the baking paper and cover with the other piece of paper. Using a rolling pin, bash the chicken breasts until they are around 1cm thick.

Heat a large, non-stick frying pan or griddle pan over a high heat. Lightly brush the chicken breasts with the sauce, then place into the pan. Cook for 3–4 minutes on each side, basting with the sauce, until the chicken is cooked through and a little caramelised, then transfer to a plate.

Toast the buns, cut-side down, for 30 seconds in the pan.

To assemble the burgers, spread the remaining 2 tablespoons of ketchup across the bottom of each bun, top with the chicken breasts, pepper, lettuce, feta and pickled jalapeños. Sandwich together to serve.

BRAISED GREEN BEANS WITH CRISPY BREADCRUMBS

VEGAN
PREP 5 MINUTES
COOK 15 MINUTES

400g trimmed green beans

3 tbsp olive oil

100g fresh white breadcrumbs

small bunch of parsley, finely
   chopped

salt and pepper

3 fat garlic cloves, finely
   sliced

1 tsp smoked paprika

4 tbsp Heinz Tomato Ketchup

100ml water

Bring a large saucepan of salted water to the boil. Add the green beans, cook for 4 minutes, then drain into a sieve.

Heat 2 tablespoons of the olive oil in a large frying pan over a medium-high heat. Add the breadcrumbs and fry for 3-4 minutes, stirring constantly, until evenly crisped and golden brown. Scrape the breadcrumbs into a bowl. Stir through the parsley and season the breadcrumbs to taste. Set aside.

Put the pan back over a medium heat. Pour in the remaining 1 tablespoon of olive oil. Add the garlic, then fry, stirring, for 1 minute until lightly golden. Add the smoked paprika, ketchup and water. Stir to create a sauce.

Tip in the green beans, then simmer away for 3-4 minutes until the beans are cooked through and coated in the sauce. Season to taste, then spoon the beans into a dish and top with the crispy breadcrumbs to serve. We like to eat this with the glazed pork chops opposite.

GLAZED
PORK CHOPS

PREP 5 MINUTES
COOK 20 MINUTES

4 good-quality pork chops
2 tsp rapeseed oil
salt and pepper
3 tbsp Heinz Tomato Ketchup
2 tbsp soy sauce
1 tbsp rice wine vinegar
1 tbsp honey

Rub the pork chops all over with oil and season on both sides with salt and pepper.

Place a large frying pan over a medium heat. Add the pork chops, fat-side down so that they are standing up in the pan. Fry this way for 5–6 minutes until most of the fat has rendered down and turned crisp.

Drain the excess fat away from the pan, then turn the pork chops meat-side down in the pan. Increase the heat to medium–high, then cook for 5 minutes on each side.

While the pork chops are cooking, mix together the ketchup, soy sauce, vinegar and honey in a small bowl.

Add the sauce to the pan and cook the pork chops for a further 3–4 minutes, basting in the sauce until sticky and cooked through. The braised green beans opposite make a brilliant side.

BACON, EGG & CHEESE CROISSANTS

SERVES 2

PREP 5 MINUTES
COOK 10 MINUTES

6 rashers smoked streaky
    bacon
4 medium free-range eggs
salt and pepper
2 croissants
30g butter
30g extra-mature Cheddar,
    grated
2 tbsp Heinz Tomato Ketchup

Preheat the oven to 160°C/140°C fan/gas mark 3.

Lay the streaky bacon rashers in a non-stick frying pan over a medium-high heat. Fry for 2–3 minutes on each side, depending on how crispy you like them.

Meanwhile, crack the eggs into a jug. Whisk well with a fork until the whites and the yolks are fully combined. Season well with salt and pepper.

Transfer the bacon to a roasting tray. Place the croissants alongside, then put both in the oven to warm while you cook the eggs.

Melt the butter in the bacon pan over a medium heat (no need to wash in between – extra flavour!). Pour in the beaten eggs. Sprinkle over the grated Cheddar, then stir the eggs. Continue moving your spoon through the entire pan every 20 seconds or so until you end up with big pieces of silky scrambled eggs.

Slice the warmed croissants in half, spread the bases with ketchup, then pile in the cheesy scrambled egg and top with the streaky bacon and serve.

FRIED RICE

VEGETARIAN
PREP 15 MINUTES
COOK 15 MINUTES

2 tbsp Heinz Tomato Ketchup

2 tbsp hot sauce (we like sriracha)

2 tbsp water

2 tbsp sesame oil, plus a drizzle to serve

4 spring onions, finely sliced (both green and white parts)

100g mangetout, halved lengthways

1 large carrot, cut into matchsticks

1 red pepper, finely sliced

2 garlic cloves, finely sliced

small piece of fresh ginger, peeled and cut into matchsticks

250g pre-cooked basmati rice pouch

2 medium free-range eggs

1 tbsp toasted sesame seeds

Mix together the ketchup, hot sauce and water in a small bowl. Set aside.

Heat 1 tablespoon of the sesame oil in a wok or high-sided frying pan over a high heat. Add most of the spring onions and all the mangetout, carrot, pepper, garlic and ginger to the pan. Stir-fry for 2–3 minutes until the veg has slightly softened.

Tip in the rice, separate the grains with the back of your spoon and mix everything together, then pour in the spicy ketchup sauce. Reduce the heat to low and leave for a few minutes to warm through.

Heat the remaining 1 tablespoon of sesame oil in a second frying pan over a high heat. Crack in your eggs and fry for 2–3 minutes until cooked to your liking. For the last 30 seconds of cooking, top the eggs with the remaining spring onions and sesame seeds.

Give the rice a good toss, season to taste, then divide between two bowls. Top each with a sesame fried egg to serve.

SECRETS OF THE SAUCE

Heinz Tomato Ketchup leaves the bottle at **0.028** miles per hour unaided (that's about the same speed as the average garden snail). The viscosity of the sauce is measured by a specially developed piece of equipment called the Quantifier. The sauce is poured into a special trough in the Quantifier set at a specific angle, and then the Heinz team check to see how far it travels in 10 seconds to ensure it's the right consistency. If the sauce is too thick or too thin, it's rejected, as every bottle has to be perfect.

Heinz Tomato Ketchup is still made using the same *secret recipe*, which has remained largely unchanged since 1907.

The recipe for the top-secret spice mix used in Heinz Tomato Ketchup is locked away in a secure vault.

GARLIC DOUGH BALLS

MAKES
9

VEGETARIAN
PREP 20 MINUTES
PLUS PROVING
COOK 15 MINUTES

7g sachet dried yeast

1 tsp caster sugar

150ml warm water

250g strong white bread flour,
   plus extra for dusting

1 tsp fine sea salt

1 tbsp olive oil, plus extra for
   greasing

100g butter

2 garlic cloves, crushed

handful of parsley, finely
   chopped (stalks and all)

**Heinz Tomato Ketchup, to
serve**

Put the yeast and sugar into a bowl. Add the warm water and stir, then leave for 5 minutes until frothy.

In a large bowl, mix together the flour and salt, then pour in the yeasty water and olive oil. Stir until a dough forms, then use clean hands to bring the dough together. Tip it out on to a lightly floured work surface and knead for 10 minutes until super smooth.

Grease a large, clean bowl with a little oil. Add the dough, then cover with a clean tea towel. Leave to rise for 1 hour, or until doubled in size.

Preheat the oven to 200°C/180°C fan/gas mark 6 and lightly oil a baking tray.

Turn out the dough on to a lightly floured work surface and knead for 1 minute. Divide into nine and use the palms of your hands to roll into even balls, the size of a golf ball. Place the dough balls on the prepared tray, spacing them out evenly. Cover and leave to rise for 30 minutes.

Bake for 12–15 minutes until lightly golden. When you tap the bottom of one, it should sound hollow.

Meanwhile, melt the butter in a small saucepan over a low heat. Add the garlic and stir through the parsley. Keep warm.

Once the dough balls are cooked, brush with the garlic butter and serve with ketchup for dunking.

SLOPPY JOES

PREP 5 HOURS
COOK 55 MINUTES

2 tbsp olive oil
500g good-quality beef mince
salt and pepper
1 onion, finely chopped
30g butter
2 fat garlic cloves, crushed
2 tsp chilli powder
6 tbsp Heinz Tomato Ketchup
1 tbsp Lea & Perrins
   Worcestershire Sauce
2 tsp soft light brown sugar
1 tbsp apple cider vinegar
200ml water
4 brioche buns, halved
pickles, to serve

Heat 1 tablespoon of the olive oil in a large frying pan over a high heat. Season the beef mince with salt and pepper, then add half the mince to the pan. Fry for 6–8 minutes, breaking down the mince with the back of your spoon, until crisp and browned. Transfer to a bowl with a slotted spoon and repeat with the remaining oil and mince.

Once all the mince has been fried and placed in the bowl, add the onion and butter to the pan (no need to wash in between – extra flavour!). Reduce the heat to medium. Cook for 8–10 minutes, stirring occasionally, until softened but not browned.

Add the garlic and cook for 30 seconds, then tip the mince back into the pan. Add the chilli powder, ketchup, Worcestershire sauce, sugar, vinegar and water. Give everything a good mix, then bring to a simmer. Leave to bubble away for 20 minutes until the mince is coated in a rich sauce. Season to taste.

Toast the buns in the toaster, then pile in the mince and top with pickles for ultimate sloppy Joes.

COD & TOMATO BAKE

PREP 10 MINUTES
COOK 25 MINUTES

2 fat garlic cloves, crushed
3 tbsp Heinz Tomato Ketchup
1 tsp dried chilli flakes, plus
    extra to serve (optional)
100ml white wine
300g cherry tomatoes on the
    vine, halved
450g jar roasted peppers,
    drained and peppers
    roughly sliced
2 x 400g tins white beans
    (we like butterbeans or
    cannellini beans), drained
salt and pepper
4 sustainably sourced
    skinless, boneless cod
    fillets
1 tbsp olive oil
4 tbsp natural yoghurt
2 tbsp capers, drained
small handful of basil leaves
crusty bread, to serve

Preheat the oven to 200°C/180°C fan/gas mark 6.

In a large bowl, mix together the garlic, ketchup, chilli flakes and white wine, then add the cherry tomatoes, roasted peppers and beans. Season well with salt and pepper, then give everything a good mix to combine.

Tip the tomato and bean mix into a large baking dish. Roughly spread out into a single layer, then roast in the oven for 15 minutes until the cherry tomatoes are beginning to break down.

Season the cod fillets on both sides, then nestle them into the baking dish. Drizzle over the olive oil, then return to the oven for 8–10 minutes until the cod is just cooked through – it should flake into large white pieces.

Drizzle the yoghurt over the dish, then scatter over the capers and basil leaves, along with a few extra chilli flakes, if you like. Serve at the table for people to help themselves, along with some crusty bread for mopping up the juices.

In the 1930s, Heinz salesmen were expected to be *'at least 6 feet tall, impeccably dressed and eloquent'*. They attended sales appointments armed with a special case containing chrome vacuum flasks filled with hot beans and soups, as well as a variety of other products to test (including ketchup, of course), as well as pickle forks and olive spears.

SERVES 4

CHERRY TOMATO RISOTTO

VEGETARIAN OPTION
PREP 5 MINUTES
COOK 40 MINUTES

2 tbsp olive oil

1 large onion, finely chopped

3 fat garlic cloves, crushed

½ tsp dried chilli flakes

300g arborio rice

2 tbsp Heinz Tomato Ketchup

400g cherry tomatoes on the vine

250ml white wine

1.2 litres hot chicken or vegetable stock

50g Parmesan or vegetarian hard cheese, finely grated

salt and pepper

handful of basil leaves

50g toasted pine nuts

Heat the olive oil in a large, high-sided frying pan over a medium heat. Add the onion, then cook, stirring regularly, for 8–10 minutes until the onion is soft but not coloured.

Add the garlic and chilli flakes, then cook, stirring, for 30 seconds. Tip in the rice and add the ketchup. Stir so that the rice gets coated in the tomatoey onions, then toast in the pan for a minute. Remove the cherry tomatoes from the vine and add them to the pan, then pour in the glass of wine.

After about 2 minutes, once the wine has been absorbed by the rice, add a ladleful of stock. Cook, stirring regularly, until the stock has been absorbed, then repeat. Keep adding the stock until most of it has been absorbed and the rice is tender with a slight bite – this will take around 20 minutes.

Add half the finely grated cheese, stir, then season the risotto to taste. Divide between four bowls, then top with the remaining cheese, the basil leaves and the toasted pine nuts, and serve.

HEINZ TOMATOES

You can't make tomato ketchup without tomatoes! The juicy, tasty vine-ripened tomatoes that are used to make Heinz Tomato Ketchup are grown in California and the Mediterranean, ensuring they get plenty of glorious sunshine.

Henry J. Heinz starting breeding tomatoes in 1934, helping to develop the unique varieties of tomato Heinz grows today. By 1957, Heinz had started producing its own tomato seeds through traditional breeding techniques, and now supplies 5 billion seeds to its farmers each year. Heinz tomatoes are redder, thicker and tastier than the tomatoes you'd generally find in a supermarket, which gives Heinz Tomato Ketchup its unique taste. The tomatoes are monitored at every stage by Heinz Tomato Masters (no, really!) to make sure the quality is tip-top.

The tomatoes are processed within hours of being picked to lock in flavour and freshness. And any tomatoes that don't pass the quality test get used in feed, compost or fertiliser, helping to grow the next delicious crop and ensuring nothing goes to waste.

Heinz uses enough tomatoes every day to full an Olympic-sized swimming pool. If all the tomatoes used by Heinz in a year were loaded into 15-tonne trucks parked end to end, they'd reach from London to Southampton.

MEATBALL PASTA BAKE

PREP 15 MINUTES
COOK 45 MINUTES

3 tbsp olive oil, plus extra for
   drizzling
1 onion, grated
salt and pepper
2 fat garlic cloves, crushed
2 x 400g tins cherry tomatoes
**2 tbsp Heinz Tomato Ketchup
   50% Less Salt & Sugar**
1 tbsp balsamic vinegar
400g fusilli
125g mozzarella, torn
green salad, to serve
   (optional)

For the meatballs
1 onion, grated
500g good-quality beef mince
**2 tbsp Heinz Tomato Ketchup
   50% Less Salt & Sugar**
2 tsp dried oregano
100g fresh breadcrumbs
1 medium free-range egg

Place all the meatball ingredients in a large bowl and, using clean hands, knead together until evenly combined. Shape into 20 small meatballs. Transfer to a tray and place in the fridge.

Heat 1 tablespoon of the oil in a saucepan over a medium heat. Add the onion, along with a pinch of salt, and cook, stirring occasionally, for 8–10 minutes until softened but not coloured. Add the garlic, then cook for a further 30 seconds. Add the cherry tomatoes, ketchup and balsamic vinegar. Stir and bring to the boil, then reduce the heat and leave to simmer away while you cook the pasta and meatballs.

Preheat the oven to 200°C/180°C fan/gas mark 6.

Bring a large saucepan of salted water to the boil. Drop in the fusilli and cook for 2 minutes less than the packet instructions, then drain into a colander.

Meanwhile, heat 1 tablespoon of the oil in a non-stick frying pan over a medium–high heat. Add half the meatballs and fry, turning regularly, for 5 minutes until browned. Transfer back to the tray and repeat with the remaining meatballs and oil.

Tip the cooked pasta into a medium baking dish. Season the sauce, then pour it over the pasta. Add the meatballs, then scatter over the mozzarella. Drizzle with a little olive oil and bake for 15–20 minutes until golden and bubbling. Serve.

PATATAS BRAVAS

VEGETARIAN
PREP 10 MINUTES
COOK 30 MINUTES

1.25kg floury potatoes (we
    like Maris Piper or King
    Edwards), peeled and cut
    into roughly 2.5cm cubes
4 tbsp olive oil
1 tbsp dried oregano
salt and pepper
1 onion, finely chopped
2 garlic cloves, crushed
2 tsp hot smoked paprika
400g tin chopped tomatoes
1 tbsp Heinz Tomato Ketchup
handful of parsley leaves
    (optional), to serve

For the cheat's aioli
1 garlic clove, crushed
4 tbsp Heinz [Seriously Good]
    Mayonnaise
zest and juice of ½ lemon

Preheat the oven to 220°C/200°C fan/gas mark 7.

Tip the cubed potatoes on to your largest roasting tray. Toss with 3 tablespoons of the olive oil, the oregano and plenty of salt and pepper, then spread out into a single layer so that the potato evenly crisps. Roast in the oven for 25–30 minutes, flipping halfway, until completely crisp and golden brown.

Meanwhile, heat the remaining 1 tablespoon of olive oil in a saucepan over a medium-high heat. Add the onion, along with a pinch of salt. Cook for 6–8 minutes, stirring regularly, until soft and a little caramelised. Add the garlic and cook for 30 seconds, then stir in the hot smoked paprika and cook for another 30 seconds. Add the chopped tomatoes and ketchup and bring to the boil, then reduce the heat to medium and leave to simmer away and reduce until the potatoes have finished roasting.

While the sauce is simmering, combine the ingredients for the cheat's aioli in a small bowl and season to taste.

Season the tomato sauce to taste. Pile the cooked potatoes into a bowl. Top with the tomato sauce, then drizzle over the aioli. Scatter over the parsley, if using, to serve.

FAMOUS FANZ

British singer Ed Sheeran is a huge fan of Heinz Tomato Ketchup. He's said to carry a bottle with him whenever he's away on tour – and in 2012 he even got a ketchup label tattooed on his arm! Now that's dedication.

In 2019, Heinz collaborated with Ed to create a limited run of 150 bottles of ketchup featuring his tattoos. Some of the bottles were auctioned off – one sold for £1,500 at Christie's Auction House, London – and the profits went to charity.

As well as this fancy tattoo-style bottle, Heinz also created a limited edition bottle of Tomato 'Edchup', featuring a tomato wearing some very familiar-looking glasses.

Ed loves the stuff so much, he even pitched and starred in a TV advert for Heinz Tomato Ketchup – in exchange for a lifetime's supply of his favourite sauce.

And Ed's not the only one – *Twilight* star Jackson Rathbone is also a huge fan, and has a Heinz Tomato Ketchup bottle tattooed on his leg.

TOMATO PILAU RICE

VEGAN OPTION
PREP 5 MINUTES
COOK 40 MINUTES

1 tbsp olive oil

1 onion, finely chopped

salt and pepper

2 fat garlic cloves, crushed

2 tsp smoked paprika

2 tsp ground cumin

1 cinnamon stick

250g long-grain rice

4 tbsp Heinz Tomato Ketchup

1 litre vegetable or chicken
   stock

100g baby spinach leaves

100g green olives, roughly
   chopped

zest and juice of ½ lemon

Heat the olive oil in a large, high-sided frying pan over a medium heat. Add the onion along with a pinch of salt. Cook for 8–10 minutes, stirring regularly, until softened but not coloured. Add the garlic and cook, stirring, for 30 seconds.

Add the smoked paprika, ground cumin and cinnamon stick. Tip in the rice, then add the ketchup. Give everything a good mix so that each grain of rice is coated in the onion, tomato and spices.

Pour in the stock. Bring the rice to a simmer, then leave to bubble away, stirring occasionally, for around 20 minutes until the rice is cooked and all of the liquid has evaporated. If the stock evaporates before the rice is cooked, top up with a little water.

Once the rice is cooked, add the spinach and olives, then stir until the spinach has wilted. Add the lemon zest and juice, then season the pilau to taste before serving.

AUBERGINE KATSU CURRY

VEGAN
PREP 20 MINUTES
COOK 50 MINUTES

2 tbsp vegetable oil, plus extra
for frying
2 onions, chopped
2 large carrots, peeled and
chopped
salt and pepper
3 garlic cloves, roughly
chopped
thumb-sized piece of fresh
ginger, peeled and roughly
chopped
1–2 tbsp medium curry
powder (depending on how
spicy you like it)
1 tsp ground turmeric
400ml tin coconut milk
2 tbsp Heinz Tomato Ketchup
50% Less Salt & Sugar
100g panko breadcrumbs
8 tbsp cornflour
100ml water
2 aubergines, sliced into 1cm-
thick rounds

*Ingredients continued on
page 62*

Heat the 2 tablespoons of vegetable oil in a medium saucepan over a medium heat. Add the onions and carrots along with a pinch of salt. Cook for 8–10 minutes, stirring regularly, until softened but not coloured.

Add the garlic and ginger to the pan. Cook, stirring, for a further minute. Spoon in the curry powder and turmeric, then cook for 30 seconds. Pour in the coconut milk, then half-fill the tin with water and add that, too. Bring the sauce to a simmer. Bubble away for 15 minutes until the veg are completely soft.

Take the sauce off the heat, add the ketchup, then blitz the sauce with a hand blender until completely smooth. Season to taste.

Tip the breadcrumbs into a wide, shallow bowl. Spoon the cornflour into a second wide, shallow bowl, then pour in the water and stir to create a milky batter; it should have a creamy consistency.

Season the aubergine rounds with salt and pepper. Working in batches, completely coat each round in the cornflour batter, then pat in the breadcrumbs to completely cover. Place the breaded aubergines on a plate. Repeat until all of the aubergine is breaded.

Preheat the oven to 120°C/100°C fan/gas mark ½.

THE TOMATO KETCHUP BOOK

AUBERGINE
KATSU CURRY
(CONTINUED)

To serve
cooked rice
freshly chopped coriander
toasted sesame seeds
(optional)
1 lime, cut into 4 wedges

Line a plate with paper towels.

Pour enough vegetable oil into a large, high-sided frying pan to cover the base by 2cm. Place the pan over a high heat until the oil is visibly shimmering. To test the temperature, drop a piece of panko into the oil – it should brown in 20 seconds but not burn.

Working in batches, carefully lower the aubergine slices into the oil. Fry for 2–3 minutes on each side until crisp and deeply golden. Using a slotted spoon, drain on the paper towels.

Transfer the cooked aubergine to a roasting tray and put in the oven to keep warm. Repeat until all the aubergine is fried.

Reheat the katsu sauce over a medium heat until warmed through. Divide the cooked rice between four bowls, then top with the aubergine slices, sauce, coriander and sesame seeds, if using. Serve with a lime wedge for squeezing over.

The katsu sauce can be made up to 2 days in advance and stored in an airtight container in the fridge.

KETCHUP FACTS

5 *June is National Ketchup Day!*

In 1962, Heinz created a recipe for a *'Love Apple Pie'* – an apple pie made with Heinz Tomato Ketchup, which was said to bring out the flavour of the apples.

The word 'ketchup' – or 'catsup', as it used to be known – is inspired by a Chinese fermented fish sauce called *koe-chiap*.

SWEETCORN & BEAN QUESADILLAS

VEGETARIAN
PREP 10 MINUTES
COOK 40 MINUTES

1 tbsp + 4 tsp olive oil
1 red onion, finely chopped
1 orange pepper, finely
    chopped
salt and pepper
1-2 tbsp Cajun seasoning
    (depending on how spicy
    you like it)
4 tbsp Heinz Tomato Ketchup
50% Less Salt & Sugar
198g tin sweetcorn, drained
400g tin kidney beans
200g cherry tomatoes on the
    vine, roughly chopped
small bunch of coriander,
    roughly chopped
½ tsp dried chilli flakes
    (optional)
zest and juice of 1 lime
8 flour tortilla wraps
100g Cheddar, grated
soured cream, to serve

Heat the 1 tablespoon of oil in a saucepan over a medium-high heat. Add the onion and pepper, along with a pinch of salt. Cook for 6-8 minutes, stirring, until softened and beginning to colour. Stir in the Cajun seasoning, then cook, stirring, for 30 seconds. Add 3 tablespoons of the ketchup, along with the sweetcorn and the kidney beans with their liquid. Stir and bring to a simmer, then leave to bubble away while you make the salsa.

In a bowl, mix together the remaining ketchup with the cherry tomatoes, coriander, chilli flakes, if using, and lime zest and juice. Season the salsa to taste, then set aside.

Roughly mash the beans with a potato masher or fork, then season to taste and take off the heat.

Preheat the oven to 100°C/80°C fan/gas mark ¼.

Heat ½ teaspoon of the olive oil in a large, non-stick frying pan over a medium heat. Place one tortilla in the pan and top with about an eighth of the bean mixture. Top with a sprinkling of Cheddar, then fold the tortilla in half. Fry for 2 minutes on each side until golden and the cheese has melted. Transfer to a baking tray and keep warm in the oven while you repeat with the remaining tortillas and filling, using ½ teaspoon of oil for each quesadilla. Once all the quesadillas are cooked, cut into triangles and serve with the tomato salsa and soured cream.

CHORIZO & PEA PAELLA

PREP 10 MINUTES
COOK 40 MINUTES

1 tbsp olive oil
225g chorizo ring, peeled and
    cut into cubes
1 large onion, finely chopped
large pinch of saffron
    (optional)
1.2 litres hot chicken stock
2 fat garlic cloves, crushed
2 tsp smoked paprika
300g paella rice
**2 tbsp Heinz Tomato Ketchup
50% Less Salt & Sugar**
450g jar roasted peppers,
    drained and roughly sliced
200g frozen peas
juice of ½ lemon, plus
    ½ lemon cut into wedges
    to serve
salt and pepper
small handful of parsley,
    roughly chopped (stalks
    and all)

Heat the olive oil in a large, high-sided frying pan over a medium heat. Add the chorizo and onion. Fry, stirring regularly, for 10 minutes until the onion is softened and the chorizo has released its oils.

Meanwhile, if using saffron, stir into the chicken stock in a bowl and leave to infuse.

Add the garlic and smoked paprika, then cook, stirring, for 30 seconds. Now add the rice and ketchup and give everything a good stir so that each piece of rice gets coated in the chorizo, onion and spices. Pour in the chicken stock and bring to the boil.

Reduce the heat to medium and leave the paella to bubble away, stirring occasionally, for around 20 minutes, until most of the stock has been absorbed and the rice is cooked with a slight bite.

Stir through the peppers and peas. Leave the peas to defrost for a couple of minutes, then squeeze in the lemon juice and season the paella to taste.

Sprinkle the parsley leaves over the paella and top with the lemon wedges. Serve at the table for people to help themselves.

KETCHUP FACTS

In the 1990s, Heinz Tomato Ketchup was officially approved by NASA for use on the International Space Station.

In 1987, **Matt LeBlanc** scored one of his first acting jobs in a TV advert for Heinz Tomato Ketchup. The ad shows him positioning a ketchup bottle on the edge of a roof, ready to pour, then heading down the stairs to the street, where he buys a hot dog from a vendor – just as the perfectly timed dollop of ketchup falls and hits his bun. Just a few years later, he landed the role of Joey in hit comedy *Friends* – and the rest is history.

In a 2004 *New Yorker* article about the history of condiments, Malcolm Gladwell wrote: 'The taste of Heinz's ketchup began at the tip of the tongue, where our receptors for sweet and salty first appear, moved along the sides, where sour notes seem the strongest, then hit the back of the tongue, for umami and bitter, in one long crescendo. How many things in the supermarket run the sensory spectrum like this?'

Rather than use colouring to make our ketchup red, Heinz just use tomatoes.

SERVES 4

TOMATO SALSA

VEGAN
PREP 10 MINUTES

1 red onion, roughly chopped
1 fat garlic clove
1 red chilli, roughly chopped
   (deseeded if you don't like
   things too hot)
small bunch of coriander,
   stalks and leaves separated
1-2 tbsp red wine vinegar
2 tbsp Heinz Tomato Ketchup
4 ripe vine tomatoes, roughly
   chopped
salt and pepper
tortilla chips, to serve

Put the onion, garlic, chilli and coriander stalks into a food processor. Pulse until very finely chopped.

Add 1 tablespoon of the vinegar and the ketchup. Pulse again to combine, then add the tomatoes and coriander leaves. Pulse again until you are left with a chunky salsa. Season with salt and pepper to taste, adding more vinegar if needed.

Serve with tortilla chips for dipping.

The salsa can be made a couple of hours in advance and kept in the fridge. Bring up to room temperature to serve.

HEINZ TOMATO KETCHUP ADVERTS THROUGH THE YEARS

1910s

Some of the earliest adverts for Heinz Tomato Ketchup focused on the importance of the ingredients.

1927

1935

1938

The king isn't the only one!

1956

Time to enjoy...
Tomato...
Tomato...
Tomato Ketchup!

Why so many 'Tomatoes'?... Simply because there are so many of them in Heinz Tomato Ketchup. Yes, two and a quarter pounds in every 12-oz. bottle! Two and a quarter pounds — to give you the richest, reddest, tastiest ketchup you could wish for!

But it takes more than just tomatoes to make *Heinz* Ketchup ... it takes all the differing, delicious flavours of selected spices and sugar, plus matured vinegar. And, most important of all, it takes Heinz to make it! Yes, only these ingredients, and the famous 'Heinz touch', can give you this so *extra-special ketchup*. No wonder it's the most popular ketchup in the country! Heinz Tomato Ketchup. 1/4 and 2/-

It's good-it's quick-it's
57 HEINZ

1958

YOU and HEINZ 57
together put 2¼lb of tomatoes on the table
to enjoy at every meal!

IT TAKES 2¼ lb. OF TOMATOES to make one 12-oz. bottle of Heinz Tomato Ketchup. Not just ordinary tomatoes, either! They've got to have a full-bodied flavour, a rich, red colour, plenty of juice and almost no seeds.

The tomatoes Heinz use are grown specially for them in Italy and ripened naturally in the warm Mediterranean sunshine. And, apart from a little sugar, matured vinegar and spices, nothing but the pure, whole goodness of 2¼ lb. of tomatoes goes into Heinz Tomato Ketchup. 1/4 or 2/-.

P.S. Don't forget there's Heinz Tomato Chutney too. It's delicious 2/6 or 2/- a bottle

It's clever to cook with ketchup...
(*Heinz, of course*)

SWISS OMELETTE

Serve savoury with a dash of Heinz Tomato Ketchup in the filling.

	Omelette:
Filling:	1 oz. butter
1 oz. butter	3 eggs
1 lb. fresh green	3 tablespoons water
peas	Salt and pepper
2 tablespoons Heinz	
Tomato Ketchup	
½ lb. grated cheese	
Salt and pepper	

STEAK ITALIENNE

Superb as a main dish—delicious with a dash of Heinz Tomato Ketchup in the cooking.

NEWEST, EASIEST way to add the luxury touch to a meal ... Heinz Tomato Ketchup IN your cooking! All the flavour of rich, red tomatoes expertly blended and spiced.

Just add a dash or two to gravies, stews—in fact, to nearly *all* your savoury dishes—for EXTRA taste that the whole family will enjoy. You can afford to experiment ... a little ketchup goes a long, long way!

Heinz
Tomato Ketchup

1962

1968

1982

Ten points if you can name this much-loved British comedian, seen here enjoying a splash of ketchup in this TV ad from the 1980s.

STICKY PORK RIBS

PREP 5 MINUTES
COOK 2¾ HOURS

2 x 500g pork rib racks
2 tbsp Cajun seasoning
salt and pepper
2 x 330ml cans of cola, sieved
3 tbsp Heinz Tomato Ketchup
1 tbsp soy sauce
1 tbsp apple cider vinegar
Ketchup Slaw (opposite), to
    serve

You will need a pastry brush.

Preheat the oven to 160°C/140°C fan/gas mark 3.

Put the pork rib racks into a large, deep roasting tin. Pat all over with the Cajun seasoning and some salt and pepper then pour in the cola. Tightly cover the tin with kitchen foil. Roast in the oven for 2 hours until juicy and tender – the meat should just come away from the bone when pressed.

Line a flat roasting tray with kitchen foil. Using tongs and a fish slice, carefully transfer the ribs to the tray. Sieve the cooking liquid into a saucepan.

Put the saucepan over a high heat, bring to the boil and then bubble away for 10 minutes until the liquid has reduced by two thirds. Add the ketchup, soy sauce and vinegar. Continue cooking for 10–15 minutes until you have a thick, sticky glaze.

Increase the oven temperature to 200°C/180°C fan/gas mark 6.

Brush the pork ribs all over with the sticky glaze. Roast the glazed pork ribs for a further 20 minutes, basting occasionally, until completely sticky and caramelised. Serve with the ketchup slaw alongside.

KETCHUP SLAW

VEGAN
PREP 5 MINUTES

6 tbsp Heinz Tomato Ketchup
3 tbsp apple cider vinegar
2–3 tsp hot sauce (we like
    sriracha), depending on
    how spicy you like it
1 tsp caster sugar
1 small white cabbage, very
    finely sliced
handful of chives, snipped
salt and pepper

Mix together the ketchup, vinegar, hot sauce and sugar in a large bowl. Add the cabbage and chives. Toss to combine so that each shred of cabbage gets coated in the dressing – using clean hands to massage the dressing into the cabbage really helps. Season with salt and pepper to taste.

This is delicious with the pork ribs opposite.

KETCHUP FACTS

For those who like the finer things in life, Heinz created a limited-edition **Ketchup Caviar** in 2019. Rather than fish eggs, this caviar used molecular gastronomy techniques to create little 'pearls' of Tomato Ketchup, each one bursting with flavour and tomatoey deliciousness. Heinz fans entered a special draw to win one of only 150 jars made for the public.

Heinz Tomato Ketchup has found its way into any number of films and TV shows over the years, including a sneaky appearance in the infamous 'I'll have what she's having' scene in the classic comedy **When Harry Met Sally**. Our favourite sauce also occupies a prominent position in the Overlook Hotel's well-stocked larder in Stanley Kubrick's **The Shining**. It pops up in the diner in **Groundhog Day,** too, while Nick Frost uses a sachet of the red stuff to play a practical joke on Simon Pegg in **Hot Fuzz**.

In 2020, Heinz created a **570**-piece jigsaw puzzle - that was made up of entirely red pieces. That'll keep you busy!

In 2021, Heinz unveiled their new **Marz Ketchup** - made using tomatoes that had been grown in the same harsh conditions found on the planet Mars. A team of astrobiologists paired with the Heinz tomato team to recreate Martian soil and growing conditions in a special biodome, before figuring out how to grow tomatoes to the same quality as those usually used in Heinz Tomato Ketchup. Once this mission had been accomplished, they marked the occasion by sending a special-edition bottle of Marz Ketchup on a space flight beyond the Earth's atmosphere. After reaching a height of 37,000 metres, the bottle returned to Heinz HQ. That's pretty out of this world!

CHILLI PANEER

SERVES 4

VEGETARIAN
PREP 20 MINUTES
COOK 30 MINUTES

3 tbsp plain flour
3 tbsp cornflour
1 tsp crushed black pepper
1 tsp chilli powder
75ml water
550g paneer, cut into large
  cubes
5 tbsp vegetable oil
1 red pepper, chopped
1 green pepper, chopped
1 large red onion, chopped
thumb-sized piece of fresh
  ginger, peeled and finely
  chopped
3 fat garlic cloves, finely
  chopped

For the sauce
1 tsp cornflour
100ml water
3 tbsp Heinz Tomato Ketchup
1 tbsp soy sauce
2–3 tbsp Indian chilli sauce
  (depending on how spicy
  you like it)
1 tsp chilli powder
1 tsp rice wine or apple cider
  vinegar

To make the sauce, mix together the cornflour and water in a bowl until you have a milky liquid. Add the ketchup, soy sauce, chilli sauce, chilli powder and vinegar. Stir well to combine and set aside.

In a large bowl, mix together the plain flour, cornflour, black pepper and chilli powder. Add the water, then whisk to form a thin batter. Add the paneer to the bowl and toss so that each cube gets completely coated.

Heat 2 tablespoons of the oil in a wok or high-sided frying pan over a medium–high heat. Once shimmering, add half the paneer. Fry, turning regularly, for 5 minutes until crisp on all sides. Transfer to a paper-towel-lined plate using a slotted spoon. Add another 2 tablespoons of oil to the pan and repeat with the remaining paneer.

Add the remaining oil to the pan, then add the peppers and red onion. Stir-fry for 5 minutes until beginning to soften, then add the ginger and garlic. Fry for a further minute, then pour in the sauce. Give everything a good stir.

Bring the sauce to a simmer. Leave the sauce to bubble away for 3–4 minutes until thickened, then add back in the crispy paneer. Give everything a good toss and cook for a further 2 minutes to reheat the paneer in the sauce before serving.

If you can't find Indian chilli sauce, you can substitute for a thick hot sauce, such as sriracha.

CHICKEN CACCIATORE

SERVES 4

PREP 5 MINUTES
COOK 1 HOUR

8 free-range skin-on, bone-in
    chicken thighs
salt and pepper
2 tbsp olive oil
2 red onions, finely sliced
2 red peppers, cut into
    medium chunks
3 fat garlic cloves, finely
    sliced
250ml white wine
4 bay leaves
a few rosemary sprigs, leaves
    stripped
4 tbsp Heinz Tomato Ketchup
250ml chicken stock
150g pitted black olives
cooked green beans and
    cooked rice or mash,
    to serve

Season the chicken thighs on both sides with salt and pepper. Heat the olive oil in a high-sided frying pan over a medium–high heat. Lay in the chicken thighs, skin-side down, and fry for 5–6 minutes until the skin is golden and beginning to crisp. Transfer to a plate.

Add the red onions and peppers to the pan. Cook for 6–8 minutes, stirring regularly, until soft and a little caramelised. Add the garlic, then cook, stirring, for 1 minute. Pour in the white wine, bring to the boil and bubble away for about 2 minutes until reduced by half.

Once the wine has reduced, add the bay and rosemary leaves, ketchup and chicken stock. Stir the sauce to combine. Return the chicken thighs, skin-side up, to the pan. Reduce the heat to medium, then leave the chicken and sauce to simmer away for 35–40 minutes until the chicken is completely cooked through.

To serve, stir through the olives and season the sauce to taste. Serve with cooked green beans and some rice or mash.

HALLOUMI FRIES

VEGETARIAN
PREP 10 MINUTES
COOK 10 MINUTES

4 tbsp Heinz Tomato Ketchup
1 ¼ tsp chilli powder
4 tbsp plain flour
2 tsp ground cumin
salt and pepper
550g halloumi, cut into fries
vegetable oil, for frying
sea salt, for sprinkling

Mix together the ketchup and ¼ teaspoon of the chilli powder in a small bowl. Set aside for dipping later.

In a wide, shallow bowl, stir together the flour, cumin and remaining 1 teaspoon of chilli powder, along with lots of salt and pepper. Add the halloumi fries and roll in the mixture until each one is evenly coated.

Preheat the oven to 120°C/100°C fan/gas mark ½. Line a plate with paper towels.

Pour enough vegetable oil into a large, high-sided frying pan to cover the base by 2cm. Heat until the oil is shimmering. You can test it is the right temperature by adding one halloumi fry to the pan and cooking for 1–2 minutes. You want it to become golden and crisp, but not burn.

Once the oil is ready, working in three batches, carefully lower the halloumi fries into the oil. Fry for 1–2 minutes until they float to the top of the oil, then using a slotted spoon, drain on the paper towels.

Transfer the cooked halloumi fries to a roasting tray and put in the oven to keep warm. Repeat with the remaining fries.

Season the fries with a little sea salt, pile into a bowl and serve with the spiced ketchup for dipping.

PRAWN NOODLE
STIR-FRY

PREP 10 MINUTES
COOK 10 MINUTES

2 tbsp soy sauce

2 tbsp Heinz Tomato Ketchup

1 tbsp dry sherry or Shaoxing
   wine

2 tbsp water

1 tbsp rapeseed or vegetable
   oil

4 spring onions, cut into
   2.5cm (1 in) pieces (both
   green and white parts)

1 green pepper, thinly sliced

small piece of fresh ginger,
   peeled and cut into
   matchsticks

2 garlic cloves, finely sliced

1 red chilli, finely sliced

2 pak choi, stalk sliced and
   leaves left whole

180g sustainably sourced
   peeled raw king prawns

300g straight-to-wok noodles

Mix together the soy sauce, ketchup, dry sherry or Shaoxing wine and water in a small bowl. Set aside.

Heat the oil in a wok or large frying pan over a high heat. Add the spring onions and pepper. Stir-fry for 2 minutes until lightly charred and beginning to soften.

Add the ginger, garlic, red chilli, sliced pak choi stalks and raw prawns to the pan. Stir-fry for a further 2–3 minutes until the prawns have turned from grey to pink.

Drop the noodles into the pan, then add the pak choi leaves and the sauce. Fry for a further minute or so, tossing everything in the sauce, until the noodles are warmed through and everything is cooked. Divide between two bowls to serve.

KETCHUP FACTS

In the Netherlands, Heinz Tomato Ketchup is enjoyed in grilled cheese sandwiches, while in Germany it's served with pasta. In Sweden, it's used as a cooking ingredient in many dishes – just like in this book.

Over **650 million** bottles of Heinz Tomato Ketchup are sold in **140** countries worldwide every year – that's more than *1,000 bottles every MINUTE.*

The No-Added Salt and Sugar Heinz Tomato Ketchup was launched in 2018. It took over six years to develop and involved more than 500 prototypes to get the flavour just right.

The Heinz factory in the Netherlands makes about **1.8 million bottles** of ketchup every day – that's about **175,000 metric tons** of ketchup a year!

Heinz Tomato Ketchup is found in three out of four UK households.

INDEX

Published in 2022 by Ebury Press an imprint of Ebury Publishing,
20 Vauxhall Bridge Road,
London SW1V 2SA

Ebury Press is part of the Penguin Random House group of companies
whose addresses can be found at global.penguinrandomhouse.com

The HEINZ trademarks are owned by H.J. Heinz Foods UK Limited
and are used under license. © 2022 H.J. Heinz Foods UK Limited

Text © Ebury Press 2022
Photography © Ebury Press 2022*
Design © Ebury Press 2022
*except images on pages 9, 10–11, 16–17, 25, 28–29, 49, 53, 57, 69 and 72–75 © Kraft Heinz

Publishing Director: Elizabeth Bond
Food Photography: Haarala Hamilton
Design: A2 Creative
Food Styling: Sophie Godwin
Food Styling Assistants: Bella Haycraft Mee and Jodie Nixon
Props Styling: Daisy Shayler Webb
Recipe Writer: Sophie Godwin
Project Editor: Tara O'Sullivan
Development: Kraft Heinz New Ventures

www.penguin.co.uk
A CIP catalogue record for this book is available from the British Library
ISBN 9781529148725

Printed and bound in Latvia by Livonia Print SIA

The authorized representative in the EEA is Penguin Random House Ireland,
Morrison Chambers, 32 Nassau Street, Dublin D02 YH68

Penguin Random House is committed to a sustainable future for our business, our readers and our
planet. This book is made from Forest Stewardship Council® certified paper.